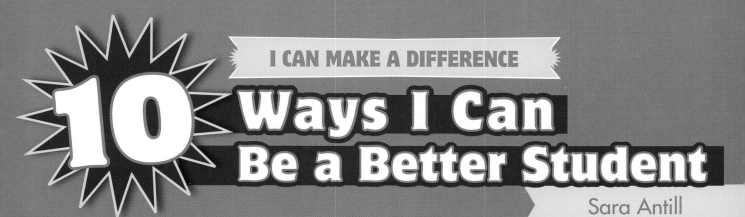

I CAN MAKE A DIFFERENCE

10 Ways I Can Be a Better Student

Sara Antill

PowerKiDS
press

New York

Published in 2012 by The Rosen Publishing Group, Inc.
29 East 21st Street, New York, NY 10010

First Edition

Editor: Jennifer Way
Book Design: Ashley Drago

Photo Credits: Cover Jupiterimages/Getty Images; pp. 4–5 Kristian Sekulic/Getty Images; pp. 6–7, 19 Shutterstock.com; pp. 8–9 Digital Vision/Thinkstock; p. 10 Hemera/Thinkstock; pp. 11, 18 Brand X Pictures/Thinkstock; pp. 12, 16–17 Stockbyte/Thinkstock; p. 13 © www.iStockphoto.com/Ls9907; pp. 14–15 Jack Hollingsworth/Photodisc/Thinkstock; p. 20 Jeffrey Coolidge/Getty Images; p. 21 Erik Isakson/Getty Images; p. 22 Jupiterimages/Comstock/Thinkstock.

Library of Congress Cataloging-in-Publication Data

Antill, Sara.
 10 ways I can be a better student / by Sara Antill. — 1st ed.
     p. cm. — (I can make a difference)
Includes index.
 ISBN 978-1-4488-6205-4 (library binding) — ISBN 978-1-4488-6369-3 (pbk.) —
ISBN 978-1-4488-6370-9 (6-pack)
 1. Study skills. 2. Academic achievement. I. Title. II. Title: Ten ways I can be a better student. III. Series.
 LB1601A58 2012
 371.3028'1—dc23

                                        2011031677

Manufactured in the United States of America

CPSIA Compliance Information: Batch #WW12PK: For Further Information contact Rosen Publishing, New York, New York at 1-800-237-9932

Contents

Learning Good Habits 4

Find a Study Buddy 6

No Distractions! 8

Make Time to Study 10

Use Your Time Wisely 11

Find a Study Spot 12

Be Prepared 13

Get Organized! 14

Write It Down 16

Ask for Help 18

Show Your Good Work 20

Teach Others! 22

Glossary 23

Index 24

Web Sites 24

Learning Good Habits

Learning is all about taking small steps. It is hard to learn multiplication before you learn addition. In the same way, it can be hard to do well in school and get good **grades** without learning good study **habits**. A habit is something that you do over and over again until it becomes natural. Good study habits are very important to have if you want to do well in school.

This book will show you 10 easy steps that you can take to become a better student. Forming good study habits in school can help you be successful in all parts of your life, both now and in the future!

Learning good study habits helps you be prepared for class.

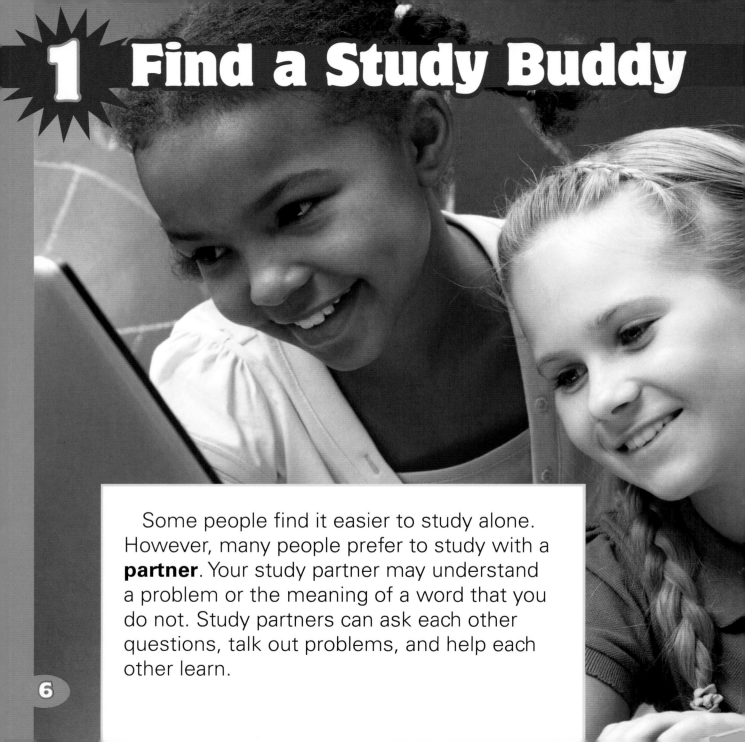

1 Find a Study Buddy

Some people find it easier to study alone. However, many people prefer to study with a **partner**. Your study partner may understand a problem or the meaning of a word that you do not. Study partners can ask each other questions, talk out problems, and help each other learn.

The easiest place to find a study partner is probably in your class. The two of you will be learning about the same subjects at the same time. You can also study with a friend from another class. His class may have talked about a subject in a way that makes more sense to you.

You and your study partner may help each other with homework. You can also quiz each other to get ready for tests.

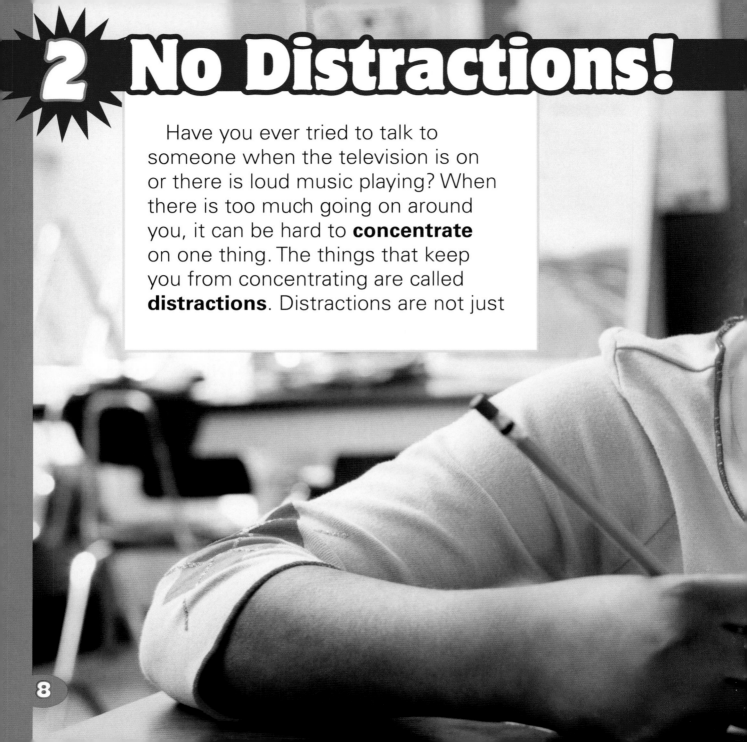

2 No Distractions!

Have you ever tried to talk to someone when the television is on or there is loud music playing? When there is too much going on around you, it can be hard to **concentrate** on one thing. The things that keep you from concentrating are called **distractions**. Distractions are not just

things that are loud. They can also be things that you are thinking about.

When it is time to study, get rid of all the distractions around you. Turn off the television and any music. This will make it easier to concentrate only on your schoolwork.

3 Make Time to Study

Having a regular study time helps make studying a habit.

By setting aside a regular time to study each day, it is easier to keep up with your schoolwork. If you get home from school at 3 p.m., try making 3:30 p.m. to 4:30 p.m. your daily study time. You can give yourself more study time or less study time as needed.

4 Use Your Time Wisely

How long does it take you to finish your homework each night? If you know you have to read for 30 minutes and do 10 math problems, do not give yourself only 15 minutes to study! Learning to plan your time out and use it wisely will help you finish your work without feeling rushed.

5 Find a Study Spot

It can be hard to study when there are other people around making a lot of noise. Try to find a quiet spot in your house where you can concentrate. If your house is just too loud, ask your parents if you can study at the **library** or another quiet place.

The library is a common study spot because it is quiet and there are few other distractions.

6 Be Prepared

Imagine you are almost finished with your homework when you realize you need a certain tool that you do not have. Before you start your homework, make a list of all the **supplies** you will need. Then make sure you have everything ready. That way, you will not have to stop to look for anything!

Make sure you have the supplies you need to do your homework. This allows you to do your work completely and correctly.

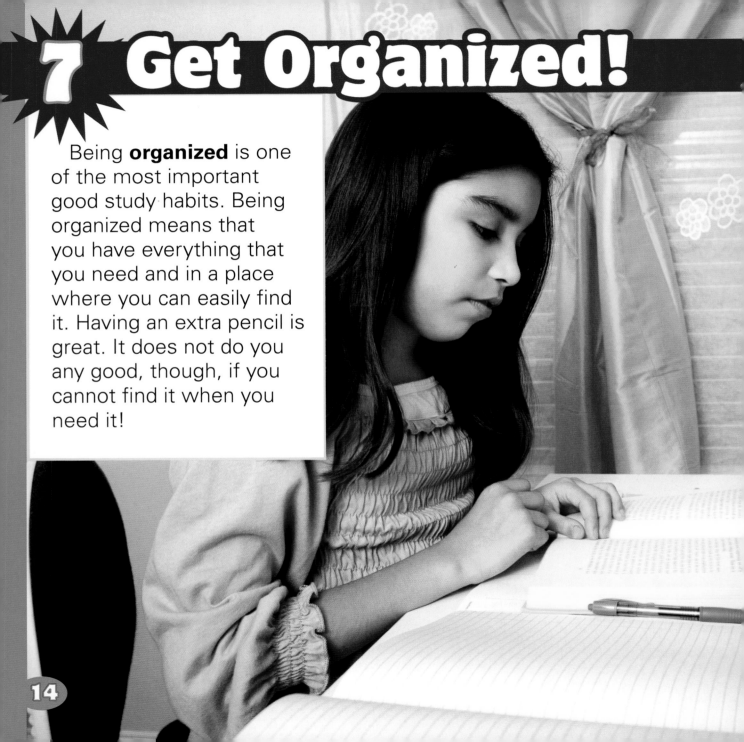

7 Get Organized!

Being **organized** is one of the most important good study habits. Being organized means that you have everything that you need and in a place where you can easily find it. Having an extra pencil is great. It does not do you any good, though, if you cannot find it when you need it!

Keeping your workspace neat helps you make sure you have the supplies you need. It also helps you concentrate on the work you are doing.

Try making a diagram of your desk or study spot. Where do you keep your pencils? Where do you keep your extra paper or your stapler? If you always keep your glue or your paper clips in a certain place, it will be easy to tell when you are running low and need more.

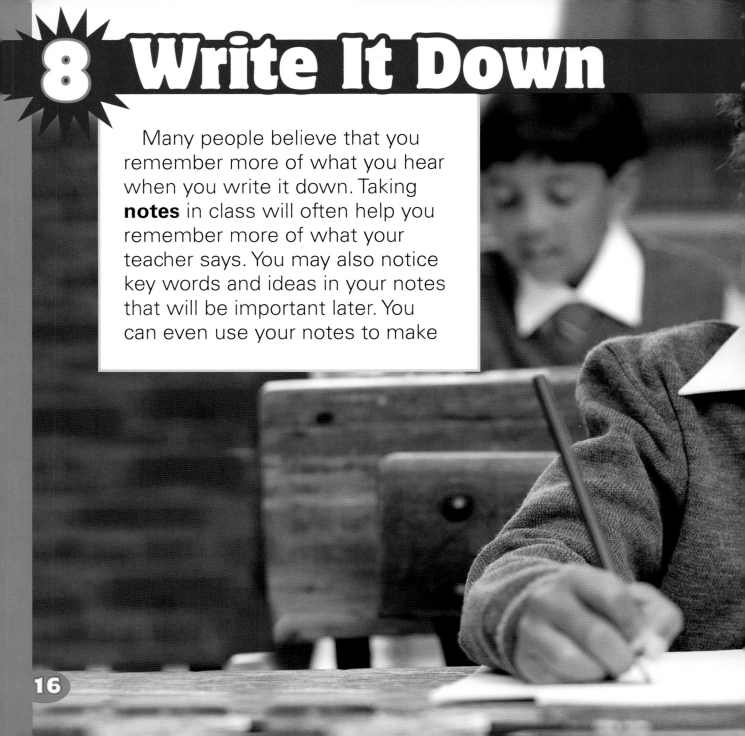

8 Write It Down

Many people believe that you remember more of what you hear when you write it down. Taking **notes** in class will often help you remember more of what your teacher says. You may also notice key words and ideas in your notes that will be important later. You can even use your notes to make

flashcards. You can study your flashcards on your own or with a friend or parent.

Writing things down can help you in a lot of ways. Write down your homework assignments each day and then read them over during your study time.

Taking notes helps you remember things more clearly. It also gives you material to look over to get ready for tests.

9 Ask for Help

Your parents may be able to help you with schoolwork that is giving you trouble. Teachers and tutors can also help you with your schoolwork or study habits.

Sometimes, even when you try your best, you may have trouble understanding a new idea. When this happens, do not be afraid to ask for help. Stay after class and let your teacher know you are having trouble. She may be able to explain the

problem in a new way. Your parents and friends may also be able to help you.

A **tutor** is a person who helps students one-on-one or in small groups. If you are having trouble in a certain subject, see if your school has a tutoring program that you can join. Libraries and **community centers** often run tutoring programs, too.

Displaying work you are proud of can help you stay motivated to keep doing well.

Doing well in school and getting good grades is something to be proud of! When you do well on a test or get a good grade on a paper, let your parents know! Many families have a spot on the wall or on the refrigerator where everyone can show off their good work.

100% ☺ (A⁺)

NAME: Lindsey #2

SPELLING TEST - UNIT # D-3

1. excite
2. above
3. relate
4. carol
5. behave
6. remind
7. poster

Being reminded that you have done well in school can help encourage you to keep doing well. The next time you do not feel like studying for a test, look at that good grade hanging on the wall. Knowing that you did well in school is a great feeling!

Getting a good grade on a test or assignment feels good and shows you that your hard work pays off!

Teach Others!

Did you know that the ideas in this book could help you be both a good student and a good study partner? The next time you study with a friend, tell him about the things that you have learned.

When your study partner has good study habits, the two of you can help each other

Study partners can teach each other good habits and study methods that work for them.

even more. Compare the notes you both took in class and see if one of you missed anything. Help each other with things you are having trouble learning. Do not forget to share your good work and encourage each other!

Glossary

community centers (kuh-MYOO-nih-tee SEN-terz) Places where activities for members of a community are held.

concentrate (KON-sen-trayt) To direct one's thoughts and attention to one thing.

distractions (dih-STRAK-shunz) Things that draw one's attention away from other things.

flashcards (FLASH-kahrdz) Cards with words, numbers, or pictures on them used to test people's knowledge.

grades (GRAYDZ) Letters or numbers that tell how well students have done.

habits (HA-bits) The usual, or common, ways people do things.

library (LY-brer-ee) A place where people go to get books, magazines, and other works.

notes (NOHTS) Written comments or explanations.

organized (OR-guh-nyzd) Having things neat and in order.

partner (PART-ner) Someone who works with another person.

supplies (suh-PLYZ) The things you need to do something.

tutor (TOO-ter) Someone who teaches one student or a small group of students.

Index

C
class, 7, 16, 18, 22

F
flashcards, 17

G
grade(s), 4, 20–21

H
habit(s), 4, 14, 22
home, 10
homework, 11, 13

L
library, 12, 19

M
multiplication, 4

N
notes, 16, 22

P
partner(s), 6–7, 22
problem(s), 6,
    11, 19

Q
questions, 6

S
school, 4, 10,
    19–21
schoolwork, 9–10
subject(s), 7, 19
supplies, 13

T
teacher, 16, 18
tutor, 19

Web Sites

Due to the changing nature of Internet links, PowerKids Press has developed an online list of Web sites related to the subject of this book. This site is updated regularly. Please use this link to access the list: www.powerkidslinks.com/diff/student/